The Blacksmith

Bobbie Kalman

Illustrations by Barbara Bedell

Crabtree Publishing

www.crabtreebooks.com

Created by Bobbie Kalman

Dedicated by Barbara Bedell

To my husband and best friend, William

Editor-in-Chief
Bobbie Kalman

Project editor
Kathryn Smithyman

Editors
Niki Walker
Amanda Bishop
Laurie Thomas

Computer design
Margaret Amy Reiach
Robert MacGregor (cover)

Production coordinator
Heather Fitzpatrick

Photo researchers
Heather Fitzpatrick
Jaimie Nathan

Consultant
Brian Gilbert
Editor, *The Hammer's Blow*
ABANA (Artist-Blacksmith
Association of North America)

Special thanks to
Old Salem, Sainte-Marie among the Hurons,
Fort George, Peter Crabtree, Marc Crabtree

Photographs
Colonial Williamsburg Foundation: 4, 8, 9, 10, 12, 26,
27, 28, 31
Photos Courtesy of Old Salem, Winston-Salem, N.C.:
page 16
Marc Crabtree at Fort George: page 30
Jim Bryant at Sainte-Marie among the Hurons:
page 14

Illustrations
All illustrations by Barbara Bedell except
the following:
Antoinette "Cookie" Bortolon: pages 17 (flatter; tongs, left),
23 (top left)
Trevor Morgan: page 10 (bottom)
Margaret Amy Reiach: page 21 (middle left)

Digital prepress
Embassy Graphics

Printer
Worzalla Publishing Company

Crabtree Publishing Company
www.crabtreebooks.com   1-800-387-7650

PMB 16A	612 Welland Ave.	73 Lime Walk
350 Fifth Ave.,	St. Catharines,	Headington
Suite 3308	Ontario,	Oxford
New York, NY	Canada	0X3 7AD
10118	L2M 5V6	United Kingdom

Cataloging-in-Publication Data
Kalman, Bobbie
    The blacksmith / Bobbie Kalman; illustrated by Barbara Bedell.
        p. cm. -- (Colonial people)
    Includes index.
    Introduces the tools, activities, and importance of the
blacksmith in colonial communities.
        ISBN 0-7787-0747-4 (RLB) -- ISBN 0-7787-0793-8 (pbk.)
    1. Blacksmithing--United States--History--17th century--
Juvenile literature. 2. Blacksmithing--United States--History--
18th century--Juvenile literature. 3. Blacksmiths--United States--
History--17th century--Juvenile literature 4 Blacksmiths--United
States--History--18th century--Juvenile literature. 5. United States--
History--Colonial period, ca 1600-1775--Juvenile literature.
[1. Blacksmithing--History. 2. Blacksmiths--History. 3. United
States--Social life and customs--To 1775.]   I. Title.
    TT220 .K29 2002
    682'.0974'09032--dc21
                                                          2001037211

Contents

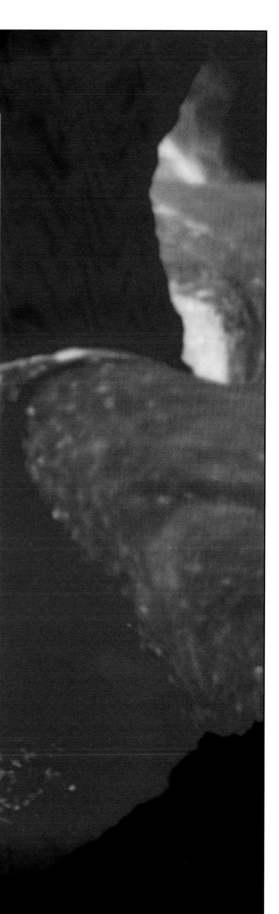

WHAT IS A BLACKSMITH?

In **colonial** times, blacksmiths made a variety of objects that people used every day. The word "blacksmith" comes from two words—"black" and "smite." Blacksmiths "smite," or pound, iron. Iron is a black metal. Iron was valuable to **colonists** because it was strong and durable. It could be **forged**, or heated and hammered, into many shapes, from cutting utensils to farming and kitchen tools.

Forming iron into various shapes required skill and hard work. An occupation that required skill was known as a **trade**. It took a colonial blacksmith several years to learn his trade. He was taught by a **master**, or expert, blacksmith.

Most blacksmiths were men, but sometimes a blacksmith's wife helped in the shop or took over the business if the blacksmith died.

Farming tools

In small towns and rural areas, the blacksmith crafted tools and **gadgets** that farmers needed. He made the metal parts of plows, hoes, and rakes—the tools that farmers used to work the land. He also repaired and sharpened these items.

Around the house

The blacksmith made many useful items for the colonial home. Most people owned iron objects such as pots and pans for cooking over an open fire. They used candleholders and lanterns for lighting their rooms and barns.

Finding a specialty

Large towns often had several blacksmiths. Some became experts at forging one type of object and were named after the objects they made. The locksmith, for example, made locks and keys, and the gunsmith made guns. The filesmith made files, which were used to smooth iron or cut notches in it.

This farmer is using a scythe to harvest grain. It has a sharp iron blade.

Cooks used iron cooking tools to make hearty meals in the fireplace.

Not just smithing

Blacksmiths known as **farriers** made shoes for animals and nailed them onto their hoofs. They were skilled at working with animals and often acted as **veterinarians**. Farriers were sometimes asked to pull out the badly decayed teeth of both animals and people! There were few dentists, and the tools farriers used for pulling nails out of hoofs were also perfect for pulling teeth.

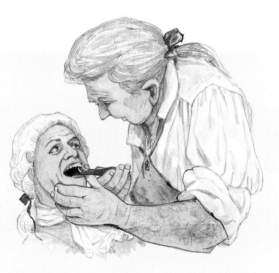

The Smithy

The village **smithy**, or blacksmith shop, was often located at the corner of two main roads so that people could find it easily. It was a busy place! Most colonists needed objects made from iron.

A place to have a chat

It was not unusual to see several people waiting at the shop while the blacksmith worked on their tools or farming equipment. No one minded waiting, however. As the blacksmith forged objects, his customers talked about the weather, politics, and town events. Some people even traded horses while waiting at the smithy.

Children's toys

Children also loved to visit the smithy. The blacksmith gave them iron hoops from old barrels or the rims from broken wagon wheels. Children raced their hoops against those of their friends. They used sticks to roll the hoops along the ground as fast as they could. When the hoops broke, they took them back to the blacksmith. The blacksmith mended them so they would roll smoothly again.

*Many Africans were brought to the colonies and forced to work as slaves. The blacksmith on the left learned his trade on a **plantation** and was given his freedom when his master died.*

THE FORGE

The most important part of the smithy was the **forge**. The forge was an open **hearth**, or fireplace, made of bricks. It was raised off the floor. The forge contained the fire the blacksmith used to heat iron. Heat made iron **malleable,** or easier to shape. A blacksmith **worked** hot iron, or changed its shape, by pounding it with a hammer. Working iron was also called **forging**.

Controlling the flames

A blacksmith had to know how to control the size and temperature of a fire. He judged the temperature by the fire's color and adjusted its heat to suit each task. A dull red fire was best for smoothing iron without changing its shape. A white-hot fire made iron the most flexible. To make the fire burn hotter, the blacksmith added more **coals** and blew air on the flames. If the fire became too hot, the blacksmith cooled it by flicking water on the coals with a bundle of twigs called a **washer**.

Fire it up

A colonial blacksmith did not have matches, so he took care not to let his fire go out. At night, he covered the hot coals with ashes. In the morning, he **stoked**, or poked, the coals and blew air on them to start the fire again.

A blacksmith used coals to make a fire because coals burned very hot.

Iron changes color as it heats up. The blacksmith could tell how hot and malleable metal was by its color. Depending on the job, he heated iron until it was red, orange, yellow, or white.

BLOW BY BLOW

Air feeds a fire and makes it burn hotter. People fanned fireplace fires using small **bellows** such as these, but the blacksmith used a huge bellows to heat the fire in his forge. A bellows was made of wood and leather. It filled with air, and when its boards were squeezed together, it blew the air into the forge.

How the bellows worked

A bellows was made up of three wide wooden boards joined together at a small **nozzle**, or narrow tube. The boards were connected to one another by large pieces of leather, which trapped air between them. The middle and top boards did not move. The bottom board was attached to a chain that connected it to a pole called a **lever**.

When the blacksmith pulled down on one end of the lever, the other end pulled up the chain and bottom board. As the board moved up, it pushed air from the lower chamber into the upper chamber through a small **valve**, or one-way opening. Air in the upper chamber was forced out of the nozzle, which was aimed at the forge. The nozzle was very narrow, so the air burst through it with great force.

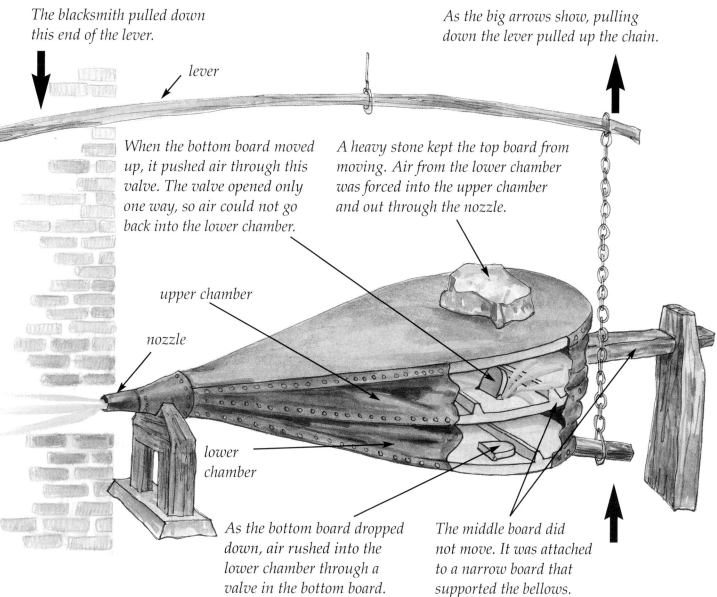

The blacksmith pulled down this end of the lever.

As the big arrows show, pulling down the lever pulled up the chain.

lever

When the bottom board moved up, it pushed air through this valve. The valve opened only one way, so air could not go back into the lower chamber.

A heavy stone kept the top board from moving. Air from the lower chamber was forced into the upper chamber and out through the nozzle.

upper chamber

nozzle

lower chamber

As the bottom board dropped down, air rushed into the lower chamber through a valve in the bottom board.

The middle board did not move. It was attached to a narrow board that supported the bellows.

11

USING THE ANVIL

Forging was a process of heating and pounding iron. A blacksmith needed a strong surface on which to hammer the hot iron to form various objects. The **anvil** was the blacksmith's work surface.

A heavy iron block

The anvil was a heavy iron block that rested on a tree trunk or a solid block of wood. An anvil could weigh up to 300 pounds (136 kg)! It was formed from solid metal. The top surface, called the **face**, had a coating of steel. Steel is much harder and more durable than iron, so it was not dented or cut when the blacksmith pounded on it.

Custom-made anvil

The anvil was the only tool that the blacksmith did not make himself. It was made for him at a **foundry**, which was a place where metal was heated at extremely high temperatures until it melted. The melted metal was poured into a **mold** and allowed to cool. The result was a tough, strong anvil.

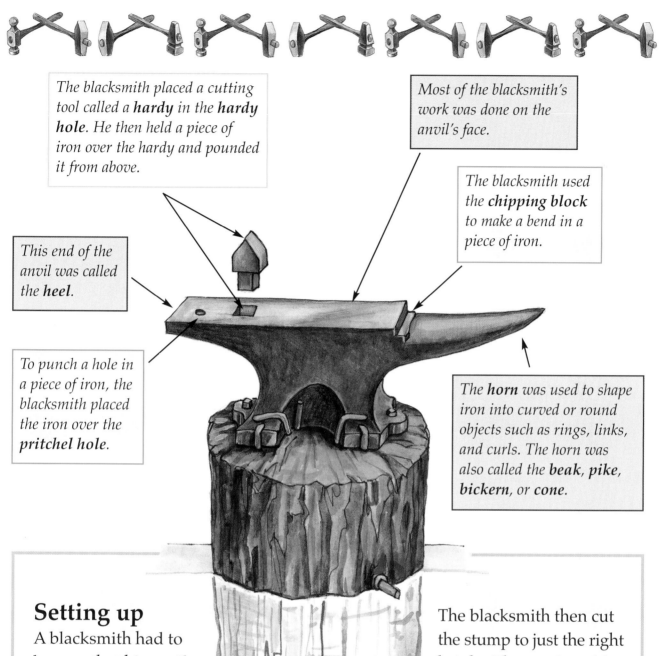

The blacksmith placed a cutting tool called a **hardy** in the **hardy hole**. He then held a piece of iron over the hardy and pounded it from above.

Most of the blacksmith's work was done on the anvil's face.

The blacksmith used the **chipping block** to make a bend in a piece of iron.

This end of the anvil was called the **heel**.

To punch a hole in a piece of iron, the blacksmith placed the iron over the **pritchel hole**.

The **horn** was used to shape iron into curved or round objects such as rings, links, and curls. The horn was also called the **beak**, **pike**, **bickern**, or **cone**.

Setting up

A blacksmith had to be sure that his anvil would not move when he hammered on it. He needed a sturdy stand to hold the anvil in place. The blacksmith selected a tall hardwood stump and sank it into a deep hole in the ground so it would not wobble.

The blacksmith then cut the stump to just the right height. The anvil could be neither too high nor too low. The blacksmith would tire quickly if he had to bend low or lift his hands too high as he hammered objects. When the stump was ready, the blacksmith attached the anvil to it with strong metal hooks.

13

AROUND THE WORKSHOP

Iron can be shaped only when it is very hot, and it cools rapidly when it is out of the fire. The anvil sat very close to the forge so that the blacksmith could pull the iron from the fire and start working it right away.

The blacksmith stood between the anvil and the forge. With a quick half-turn, he swung the iron from the fire to the anvil. When the iron cooled, he turned back to the fire. He repeated these movements many times during a day.

Too hot to handle!

Heated iron was far too hot for the blacksmith to hold in his bare hands. To avoid burning himself, he held the iron with a pair of long-handled **tongs**. Even the handles of the tongs became hot after a while!

Cool it!

When the blacksmith needed to cool a piece of iron, he **quenched** it by plunging it into a tub of water that sat near the forge. He also cooled his tongs so that they would not burn his hands.

A forge was made of bricks because bricks did not catch fire. A hood near the forge sucked smoke up the chimney.

The bellows was either on the floor next to the forge or mounted above it.

The blacksmith's tools were always within easy reach.

A bucket of water stood nearby for quenching hot iron.

The blacksmith used a vise to hold hot iron in place.

USING DIFFERENT TOOLS

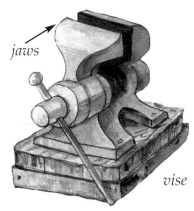

jaws

vise

The blacksmith used many kinds of tools to work metal into various shapes. Before starting each job, he organized the tools he needed on his workbench. The blacksmith did not want to waste time looking for the tools he needed while he worked. He used several kinds of hammers, tongs, and vises. A vise has two adjustable jaws to hold a piece of hot iron securely. The blacksmith above is using a vise to hold an object so he can file it smooth.

Most blacksmiths had twelve types of hammers. The different hammers allowed the blacksmith to make objects of almost any size or shape. The blacksmith kept his tools organized on his workbench, shown left.

The blacksmith made each pair of tongs for a specific purpose, such as holding round, square, or flat objects.

face →

*The blacksmith shaped curved objects such as pots, ladles, and cups by tapping them with the round peen of a **ball peen hammer**.*

← peen

*Iron was pounded flat with a **flatter**. The flatter's smooth face did not dent the iron.*

*The blacksmith used a heavy **sledge** to strike objects with great force.*

*The blacksmith used a **set hammer** to cut or make a bend in a piece of iron. He put the iron on the chipping block, placed the set hammer on the iron, and pounded the hammer with a sledge.*

*A **chisel** was used to cut iron. The blacksmith positioned the chisel on the iron and then pounded the chisel with a sledge.*

17

STEPS IN FORGING

There were several basic steps in the process of forging. Depending on what he was making, the blacksmith added or skipped some of the steps. He used several steps to forge a door hinge but only a few to make a nail. Six basic steps were needed to make a kitchen ladle. They are shown on these pages.

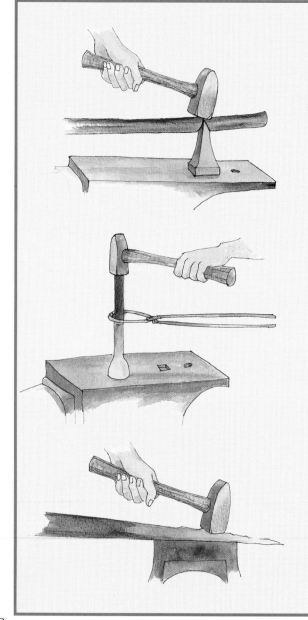

1. Cutting
The blacksmith started by cutting a cold iron bar to the length of a ladle using the hardy. He held the bar against the hardy and hit it with a hammer. When the iron was cut half-way through, the blacksmith flipped it over and hit it on the opposite side to weaken it. He then broke the bar with his hands.

2. Upsetting or upending
To make the ladle's scoop, the blacksmith heated one end of the rod to form a lump. He then held the rod upright with the hot end against the anvil. He pounded the cold end with a hammer to **upset** the hot end, or force it to thicken.

3. Drawing out
A ladle's handle had to be thin enough to grasp. The cold end was heated and **drawn out** to make it thinner. The blacksmith heated the rod, placed it on the anvil, and pounded it. While he pounded the rod, he rotated it to make sure the handle would be the same thickness all the way around.

4. Forming

a) The blacksmith had to flatten the upset end of the rod. He pounded the lump with the face of a hammer until it was flattened into a round shape. He then forged this round part into a scoop. He heated the flattened end of the rod again and used the peen end of his hammer to make a curved dent in it.

b) The blacksmith continued to hit the scoop with the peen until it was totally rounded. When the spoon was fully shaped, the blacksmith smoothed the ladle's handle with a file.

5. Bending

The blacksmith made a finger-sized loop at the end of the handle so the ladle could be held or hung up easily. He heated the end and hammered it around the horn of the anvil to curve it.

6. Hardening

When the blacksmith finished shaping and smoothing the ladle, he made it stronger by **hardening** it. He repeatedly heated the ladle and then plunged it into cold water. Heating and cooling the ladle a few times made the iron strong and durable.

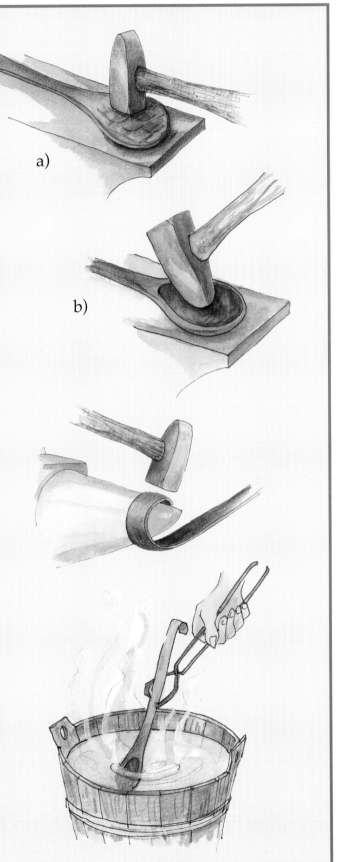

a)

b)

GADGETS FOR THE HOME

Blacksmiths made many of the tools and gadgets found throughout a colonial home. Utensils made of iron lasted many years. People cooked in an open fireplace, so pots and kitchen tools had to be sturdy enough to withstand fire without burning or melting. The pictures on these two pages show many iron gadgets that were used in a colonial home. Besides pots, pans, and cooking utensils, families purchased lanterns, hooks, door hinges, and shoe scrapers, such as the one below, from the blacksmith. People needed to scrape dirt off their shoes before they entered a house. Unpaved roads became muddy when it rained, and horses and other animals left droppings where people walked.

Safer cooking

At first, many household utensils were made from wood. The early colonial cook hung her pot over the fire on a thick, wooden **lugpole**. The lugpole eventually became dry and brittle over the fire and often broke. Blacksmiths began to make iron **cranes**, shown below, to replace lugpoles. Cranes were much safer. They did not break easily, and they allowed the cook to swing a pot in and out of the fireplace to stir a stew while it cooked.

Fireplace tools

Pots and kettles were hung from the crane by thick hooks called **trammels**. A stew cooked slowly in a pot hung high above the fire on a short trammel. If the cook wished to boil water, she used a longer trammel to move the kettle closer to the fire.

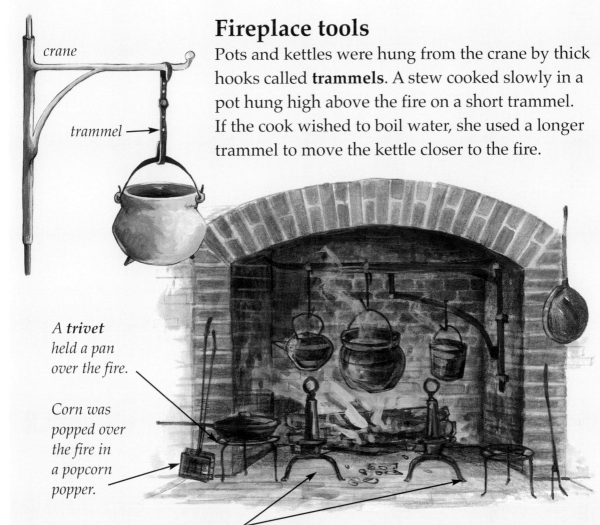

crane

trammel →

*A **trivet** held a pan over the fire.*

Corn was popped over the fire in a popcorn popper.

***Andirons**, or "fireplace dogs," were iron stands that held burning logs.*

Iron Tools for Farmers

Farming was an important activity—and a lot of hard work. Many families grew their own fruits and vegetables. They also raised livestock for milk, meat, and to help with farm work. Farmers used a variety of hand tools to prepare the land for planting, to tend plants during growing seasons, and to harvest the crops as they ripened.

Farming tools included plows, shovels, scythes, sickles, and hoes. Farmers carved their own wooden tool handles to fit their hands, but they relied on the blacksmith to make the iron parts, such as the cutting edges. The blacksmith also made chains for harnessing animals, ax blades for chopping down trees, and hinges and latches for securing gates and barn doors.

Hinges attached heavy barn doors to door frames, allowing them to swing open and closed. Iron nails fastened the hinges to the wooden frames.

The farmer used a **cradle** to cut down grain at harvest time.

Iron handles and latches were used to open and close doors, drawers, and bins.

Hoes had sharp flat blades that broke up the hard soil to prepare it for planting crops.

Axes were used to cut down trees and chop firewood. The blacksmith forged the sharp ax head.

Farmers used a curved blade called a **sickle** to cut tall grass, hay, and corn stalks.

The essential plow

The farmer's main tool was the plow. A plow had an iron **plowshare**, or blade, which was attached to a wooden frame. Oxen or horses pulled the plow, and the farmer walked behind to steer it. The plowshare cut **furrows**, or ridges, into the soil. The farmer and his family then planted seeds in the furrows to grow crops such as corn and beans.

plowshare

23

WORKING WITH ANIMALS

When horses and oxen walked on hard surfaces, such as cobblestones, their hoofs wore down. Farriers made iron shoes for these animals to wear on their hoofs. They **shod**, or shoed, the animals by nailing the shoes onto their hoofs to cover and protect them, just as shoes protect your feet.

In winter, farriers shod animals with shoes that had studs on the bottom. Studs gave animals a better grip as they pulled sleighs over slippery snow and ice. Farriers that were very good at working with animals also acted as veterinarians by caring for animals that were sick or ready to give birth.

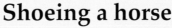

Shoeing a horse

1. Nervous horses often kicked, so the farrier's first job was to relax the animal. Once the horse was calm, the farrier lifted its leg and cradled its hoof in his lap.

2. Next, he gently loosened and removed the nails from the old shoe and pulled it off. Once the hoof was bare, he cleaned the mud and stones out of it.

3. When all the shoes were off, the farrier cut away the dead ends of each hoof, just as you clip the ends of your fingernails.

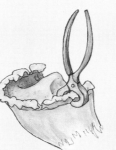

4. To make the shoes, the farrier cut an iron rod into four pieces. He heated each piece in the forge and bent it into a wide curve by hammering it over the horn of the anvil.

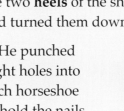

5. The farrier forged a **cat's ear** at the front of each shoe. The cat's ear protected the front edge of the hoof and stopped the shoe from slipping. The farrier then heated the two **heels** of the shoe and turned them down.

6. He punched eight holes into each horseshoe to hold the nails.

7. The farrier fitted the shoes to the horse's hoofs while the shoes were hot. The malleable shoes molded to fit the hoofs perfectly. The hot shoes did not hurt the horse. When all the shoes were made, the blacksmith hung them over the horn of the anvil to cool.

8. He used special nails to hammer the shoes onto the hoofs. The short nails did not hurt the horse.

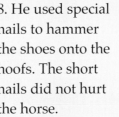

9. When the horse was shod, the small nails showed on the upper part of its hoof.

nail

cat's ear

heel

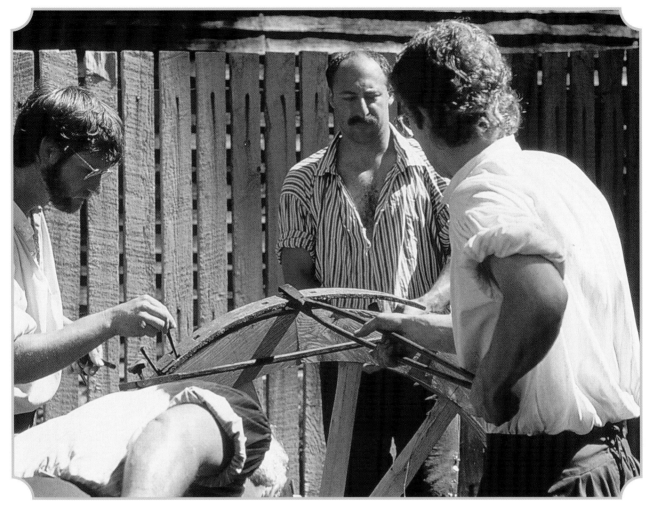

Tools for the Trades

The blacksmith was not the only tradesperson in a colonial village. **Coopers** made barrels, **wheelwrights** made wheels, and **harnessmakers** made harnesses, saddles, and bags from leather. These tradespeople and others used iron tools made by the blacksmith. They also needed iron parts for the products they created. Many hired blacksmiths to work right in their shops.

The wheelwright

A wheel was made mostly of wood, but iron rings were added to its rim and **hub**, or center, to make it stronger. The hub held a dozen or more spokes in place. Inside the hub was an iron **axle** that connected two wheels and caused them to turn. An iron hoop called a **tire** circled the wooden rim snugly and made the wheel sturdier. The men shown above are **ironing** a wheel, or putting a tire on it.

Harnessmakers

A harnessmaker was important to anyone who traveled. He made the harnesses, saddles, and **bridles** people used when riding horses. These items were made mostly of leather, but a blacksmith made their iron parts.

An important part of a bridle was the iron **bit**, which rested in the horse's mouth. The rider used it to control the animal. The blacksmith also made metal foot holders called **stirrups** for leather saddles.

The blacksmith forged many of the harnessmaker's tools. He made iron **awls**, which were pointed tools that harness-makers used to poke holes in leather. He also made the sharp blades that the harnessmaker used to cut leather.

awl holes

iron stirrup

← *bit*

Making barrels

A cooper made barrels, buckets, and other containers using planks of wood called **staves**. The staves were arranged side by side to create a **cylinder**. They were then pulled together tightly to form a barrel. The cooper fastened the staves by putting iron hoops around the barrel. The strong, tight rings made the barrel leakproof and long-lasting. Hoops were made in many sizes to fit different containers. In large towns, coopers employed their own blacksmiths. In small communities, a cooper paid the village blacksmith to forge the hoops.

The hoops had to fit the staves tightly, so getting them on was often a difficult process!

OTHER METALWORKERS

Silversmiths, goldsmiths and gunsmiths were other types of colonial metalworkers. The smiths were named for the metals they used or the items they made. Smiths heated metal and hammered it into various shapes. The forging techniques used by other smiths were similar to those used by the blacksmith.

tankard

A silversmith, shown above, made bowls, silverware, teapots, and **tankards** from silver. He also sold and repaired watches, shoe buckles, silver buttons, and jewelry. People could take silver coins, spoons, and other items to a silversmith to have them melted. After melting the silver, the silversmith smoothed it into flat sheets. He hammered and shaped the sheets into new objects for his customers. Sometimes the smith engraved special designs or initials into objects to help identify them when they were stolen.

Keeping up appearances

Not everyone could afford gold or silver. A whitesmith crafted beautiful iron objects that looked similar to those made by goldsmiths and silversmiths. He used a file to smooth iron items such as indoor lamps and serving spoons until they were shiny and light in color.

file

lantern

The gunsmith

A gunsmith made and assembled both the wooden and metal parts of a gun. He was skilled at carving and shaping the intricate wooden handles called **stocks**. He was known as a "smith" because he forged the metal **barrels** and **triggers** for his guns. He then assembled the parts of the gun.

Founders

Not all metalworkers were smiths. Founders did not pound metal. They poured **molten**, or melted, metal into molds and left it to cool and harden. The molds shaped the metal into items such as keys, candlesticks, and buckles. Some molds also left intricate designs on the item's surface. The founder often created molds for other metalworkers. Some founders **smelted**, or melted and blended, different metals to make items of bronze, pewter, and brass from metals such as copper, zinc, tin, and lead.

LIFE AS AN APPRENTICE

Every blacksmith learned his trade as an **apprentice** and trained at least one young apprentice himself. An apprentice was a youth who assisted a tradesperson and eventually learned his or her trade. Most fathers decided which trades their sons would learn, and they chose the tradespeople who would teach them. Boys could be apprenticed to coopers, printers, wheelwrights, and blacksmiths. Instead of apprenticing, most girls learned skills such as cooking, spinning, and sewing. A few girls, however, became milliner or wigmaker apprentices.

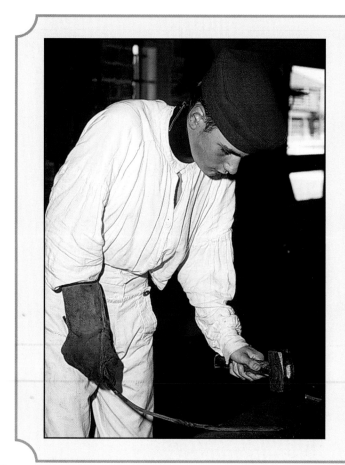

Signing the contract

Before a blacksmith took on an apprentice, both he and the young man signed an **indenture**, or contract. By signing the contract, the apprentice agreed to work for the blacksmith for up to six years without pay. In return, the blacksmith promised to teach the apprentice the "mystery," or skills, of his trade.

Learning important skills

For his first two years, the apprentice did not work with iron at all. Instead, he hauled coal, ran errands, and cleaned the shop. He also learned how to read, write, and work with numbers. He needed these skills to run a business. The blacksmith then taught his apprentice how to forge items. The apprentice often developed forging skills by starting with small objects such as nails.

Becoming a journeyman

At the end of his indenture, the apprentice became a **journeyman**. Unlike an apprentice, a journeyman was paid for his work. The blacksmith gave him a set of tools, new clothes, and a small sum of money. A journeyman had an important choice to make. He could leave the blacksmith to work for another tradesperson, travel from place to place repairing broken items, or stay on and work for the blacksmith who trained him.

Training new apprentices

If the journeyman decided to stay on with his teacher, he often helped the blacksmith train new apprentices. He also worked as a **striker**, or hammerman. A striker was used for large, two-person jobs such as making axles. He pounded the hot iron with a sledge while the blacksmith shaped it.

GLOSSARY

anvil A heavy iron block on which the blacksmith hammered iron

axle A rod under a vehicle that connects a pair of wheels and allows them to turn

barrel The metal tube of a gun through which a bullet travels

bellows A gadget made of wood and leather that is squeezed to force air onto a fire

bridle A harness that fits over an animal's head and includes a bit and reins

coal Fuel for fire, produced by slowly burning wood into small, hard pieces

colonial Relating to living in a colony or to a period when European countries ruled North America

colonist A person who lives in a colony

colony An area ruled by a faraway country

cylinder A round tube shape

face The hard, flat surface of an anvil

farrier A person who made and attached iron shoes to animal hoofs

forge (n) A large open fireplace used by a blacksmith to heat iron; (v) To heat, pound, and shape iron

gadget A small device that performs a simple job such as cutting or grinding

hardy A tool that was set in an anvil upon which iron was cut

horn The cone-shaped end of an anvil, used to shape iron into curves

malleable Describing something that can be bent and shaped easily

mold A hollow form into which melted metal is poured to harden into a certain shape

plantation A large farm with one main crop

quench To cool by dipping into water

smithy A blacksmith's workshop

tongs A tool used to grip iron, made up of two pieces joined at one end

trade A job requiring skill

trigger The part of a gun that is pulled to fire a bullet

veterinarian A person who cares for sick and injured animals

vise A clamping tool used to hold a piece of iron tightly so that it will not move

washer A bundle of sticks used for flicking water onto coals in order to cool them

INDEX

1 2 3 4 5 6 7 8 9 0 Printed in the U.S.A. 1 0 9 8 7 6 5 4 3 2